USING
MATHS
MISSION INTO SPACE

by Hilary Koll, Steve Mills
and Anne Brumfitt

ticktock

USING
MATHS
MISSION INTO SPACE

Copyright © ticktock Entertainment Ltd 2006

First published in Great Britain in 2006 by ticktock Media Ltd.,
Unit 2, Orchard Business Centre, North Farm Road, Tunbridge Wells, Kent, TN2 3XF

ISBN 1 86007 988 1
Printed in China

HILARY KOLL

Hilary Koll (B.Ed. Hons) was a Leading Maths Teacher in a primary school before training as a Numeracy Consultant for the National Numeracy Strategy. She has worked as a Lecturer in Mathematics Education at the University of Reading, teaching on undergraduate, post-graduate and training courses. She is now a full-time writer and consultant in mathematics education. Hilary Koll and Steve Mills can be contacted via their website www.cmeprojects.com

STEVE MILLS

Steve Mills (B.A. Hons, P.G.C.E., M.Ed.) was a teacher of both primary and secondary age children and an LEA Maths Advisory Support Teacher before joining the University of Reading as a Lecturer in Mathematics Education. He worked with both under-graduate and post-graduate students in their preparation for teaching maths in schools. He has written many mathematics books for both teachers and children. Visit www.cmeprojects.com for details.

ANNE BRUMFITT

Anne Brumfitt, BA Hons (London), PGCE, has a wide and extensive background across the UK and Europe in formal and informal education as a classroom teacher, examiner and specialist education consultant. She is presently Education Consultant to the European Space Agency Directorate of Science in Noordwijk, Netherlands. Anne believes space is a wonderful genre to inspire young people.

CONTENTS

NUMERACY WORK COVERED IN THIS BOOK:

CALCULATIONS:
Throughout this book there are opportunities to practise **addition, subtraction, multiplication** and **division** using both mental calculation strategies and pencil and paper methods.

NUMBERS AND THE NUMBER SYSTEM:
- COMPARING NUMBERS: pgs. 6, 7, 15, 25
- DECIMALS: pgs. 10, 17, 18, 19
- FRACTIONS: pg. 20
- NEGATIVE NUMBERS: pgs. 12, 14, 15
- NUMBER SEQUENCES: pgs. 10, 21, 22
- ORDERING NUMBERS: pg. 7
- PERCENTAGES: pgs. 20, 21
- ROUNDING NUMBERS pgs. 17, 19, 27

SOLVING 'REAL LIFE' PROBLEMS:
- READING DIALS AND SCALES: pg. 12
- TIME: pgs. 8, 9, 11, 17, 19, 20, 21, 26, 27

HANDLING DATA:
- AVERAGES: pg. 17
- CHARTS: pgs. 16, 17, 25
- ESTIMATING: pgs. 6, 7
- GRAPHS: pg. 15
- PIE CHARTS: pgs. 20, 21
- PROBABILITY: pg. 24
- TABLES: pgs. 6, 7, 17, 25
- USING FORMULA: pgs. 18, 23

SHAPE AND SPACE:
- 3-D SHAPES: pg. 6
- GRID CO-ORDINATES: pg. 13

Supports the maths work taught at Key Stage 2 and 3

HOW TO USE THIS BOOK

Maths is important in the lives of people everywhere. We use maths when we play a game, ride a bike, go shopping – in fact, all the time! Everyone needs to use maths at work. You may not realise it, but an astronaut would use maths to travel into space! With this book you will get the chance to try lots of exciting maths activities using real life data and facts about NASA and the International Space Station. Practise your maths and numeracy skills and experience the thrill of what it's really like to be an astronaut.

This exciting maths book is very easy to use – check out what's inside!

Fun to read information about Mars and the steps that are needed to undertake a manned mission there.

MATHS ACTIVITIES

Look for the
MISSION TASK.
You will find real life maths activities and questions to try.

To answer some of the questions, you will need to collect data from a DATA BOX. Sometimes, you will need to collect facts and data from the text or from charts and diagrams.

Be prepared! You will need a pen or pencil and a notebook for your workings and answers.

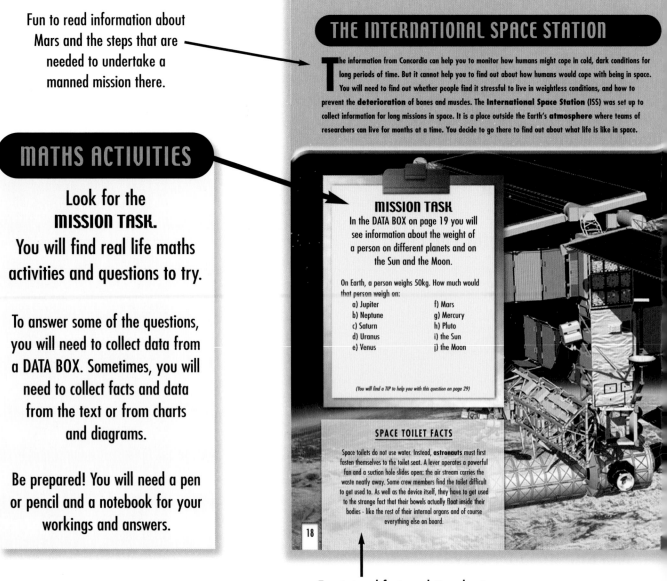

THE INTERNATIONAL SPACE STATION

The information from Concordia can help you to monitor how humans might cope in cold, dark conditions for long periods of time. But it cannot help you to find out about how humans would cope with being in space. You will need to find out whether people find it stressful to live in weightless conditions, and how to prevent the **deterioration** of bones and muscles. The **International Space Station** (ISS) was set up to collect information for long missions in space. It is a place outside the Earth's **atmosphere** where teams of researchers can live for months at a time. You decide to go there to find out about what life is like in space.

MISSION TASK
In the DATA BOX on page 19 you will see information about the weight of a person on different planets and on the Sun and the Moon.

On Earth, a person weighs 50kg. How much would that person weigh on:
  a) Jupiter   f) Mars
  b) Neptune   g) Mercury
  c) Saturn   h) Pluto
  d) Uranus   i) the Sun
  e) Venus   j) the Moon

(You will find a TIP to help you with this question on page 29)

SPACE TOILET FACTS
Space toilets do not use water. Instead, **astronauts** must first fasten themselves to the toilet seat. A lever operates a powerful fan and a suction hole slides open: the air stream carries the waste neatly away. Some crew members find the toilet difficult to get used to. As well as the device itself, they have to get used to the strange fact that their bowels actually float inside their bodies - like the rest of their internal organs and of course everything else on board.

18

Fun to read facts and tips about space.

DATA BOX

If you see one of these boxes, there will be important data inside that will help you with the maths activities.

MATHS ACTIVITIES

Feeling confident?
Try these extra
CHALLENGE QUESTIONS.

ISS FACTS

- The ISS travels around the Earth about 400 km above our heads.
- It orbits the Earth at 28 000 km per hour, which is about 7.8 km every second.
- The ISS takes only 1.5 hours to orbit the Earth.

DATA BOX GRAVITY

A person's weight changes as they go to different planets, as **gravity** is different on each planet.

On Jupiter a person's weight is about 2.63 times their weight on Earth.
On Mars a person's weight is about 0.38 times their weight on Earth.
On Mercury a person's weight is about 0.34 times their weight on Earth.
On Neptune a person's weight is about 1.4 times their weight on Earth.
On Pluto a person's weight is about 0.13 times their weight on Earth.
On Saturn a person's weight is about 1.13 times their weight on Earth.
On Uranus a person's weight is about 1.06 times their weight on Earth.
On Venus a person's weight is about 0.87 times their weight on Earth.

On the Sun a person's weight would be about 279 times their weight on Earth.
On the Moon a person's weight is about 0.17 times their weight on Earth.

An artist's impression of how the International Space Station looks from space.

CHALLENGE QUESTIONS

The ISS **orbits** the Earth at 28 000 km per hour. To help you understand how fast this is, you can compare it with other moving objects. You will need a calculator to answer these questions. Round your answers to the nearest whole number.

A person walks at 8 km per hour. This is 8000 metres per hour, 133 metres per minute and 2 metres per second. Now try these questions:
1) A person runs at 12 km per hour. What is this in
   a) metres per hour?   b) metres per minute?   c) metres per second?
2) A car on a motorway travels at 108 km per hour. What is this in
   a) metres per hour?   b) metres per minute?   c) metres per second?
3) An express train travels at 240 km per hour. What is this in
   a) metres per hour?   b) metres per minute?   c) metres per second?
4) An aeroplane travels at 960 km per hour. What is this in
   a) metres per hour?   b) metres per minute?   c) metres per second?
5) The ISS travels at 28000 km per hour. What is this in
   a) metres per hour?   b) metres per minute?   c) metres per second?

(You will find a TIP to help you with these questions on page 29)

19

IF YOU NEED HELP...

TIPS FOR MATHS SUCCESS

On pages 28 – 29 you will find lots of tips to help you with your maths work.

ANSWERS

Turn to pages 30 – 31 to check your answers.
(Try all the activities and questions before you take a look at the answers.)

GLOSSARY

On page 32 there is a glossary of astronomy words and a glossary of maths words. The glossary words appear **in bold** in the text.

THE PLANET MARS

Mars is an amazing planet. People believe it is more like Earth than any of the other planets. It is smaller than Earth but people have always wondered whether humans could ever live there. Its surface is impressive, with towering mountains and deep craters. The highest mountain on Mars is actually a volcano. It has been named Olympus Mons. Mars is covered in dust, the result of billions of years of erosion by Martian winds. There is so much dust that it has blown into dunes at the North Pole! In other places the wind has blown the dust away leaving bare rock. Mars is further away from the Sun than Earth and is a cold, dry place. Find out more about it on this page.

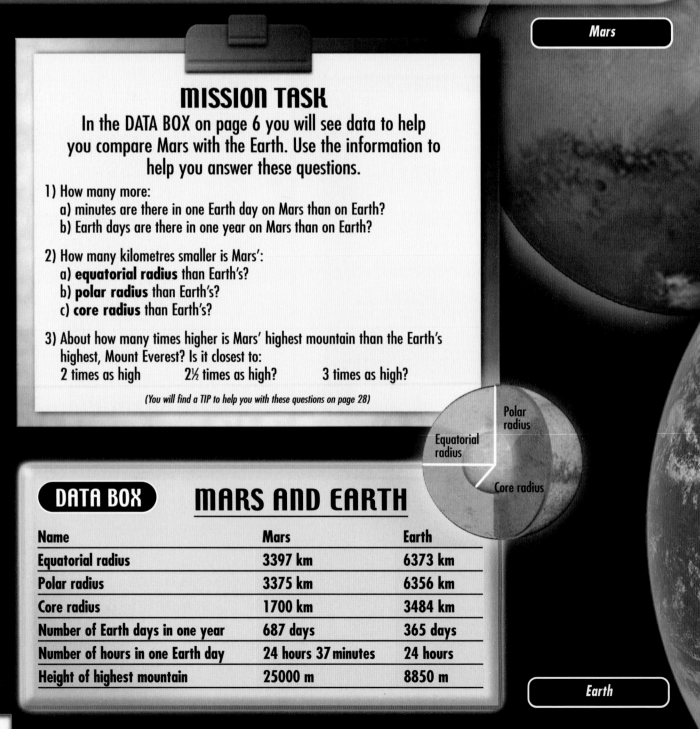

Mars

MISSION TASK
In the DATA BOX on page 6 you will see data to help you compare Mars with the Earth. Use the information to help you answer these questions.

1) How many more:
   a) minutes are there in one Earth day on Mars than on Earth?
   b) Earth days are there in one year on Mars than on Earth?

2) How many kilometres smaller is Mars':
   a) **equatorial radius** than Earth's?
   b) **polar radius** than Earth's?
   c) **core radius** than Earth's?

3) About how many times higher is Mars' highest mountain than the Earth's highest, Mount Everest? Is it closest to:
   2 times as high   2½ times as high?   3 times as high?

(You will find a TIP to help you with these questions on page 28)

Polar radius

Equatorial radius

Core radius

DATA BOX   MARS AND EARTH

Name	Mars	Earth
Equatorial radius	3397 km	6373 km
Polar radius	3375 km	6356 km
Core radius	1700 km	3484 km
Number of Earth days in one year	687 days	365 days
Number of hours in one Earth day	24 hours 37 minutes	24 hours
Height of highest mountain	25000 m	8850 m

Earth

Mars is sometimes called the Red Planet because of its colour. Mars is red because of the oxidized iron in its soil and rocks.

*Plans are being made to send **astronauts** to Mars by the year 2030.*

DATA BOX ▶ DISTANCE FROM THE SUN

All the planets in our **solar system** revolve around the Sun.

This chart shows average distances from the Sun (rounded to nearest million km).

Earth	150 million km
Jupiter	778 million km
Mars	228 million km
Mercury	58 million km
Neptune	4497 million km
Pluto	5900 million km
Saturn	1427 million km
Uranus	2870 million km
Venus	108 million km

CHALLENGE QUESTIONS

Use the information in the DATA BOX on page 7 to help you answer these questions.

1) List the planets in order of their average distance from the Sun, from the one closest to the one furthest away.

2) Which planet is usually closest to the Earth?

3) How much nearer is Mars to the Sun than:
   a) Jupiter is to the Sun?
   b) Saturn is to the Sun?
   c) Neptune is to the Sun?

4) Which planet is:
   a) about seven times further from the Sun than Venus?
   b) about four times further from the Sun than Mercury?
   c) about forty times further from the Sun that Earth?
   d) over one hundred times further from the Sun that Mercury?

(You will find a TIP to help you with these questions on page 28)

PLANET FACTS

A year in a planet's life is the time it takes the planet to make one complete **orbit** around the Sun. A day in a planet's life is the time it takes the planet to make one complete revolution or rotation about its own axis.

HUMANS ON MARS

The space agency you work for is thinking of sending a manned mission to Mars in the future. But before they can do this, they need to find out a lot more about Mars. Your space agency decides to send a robotic spacecraft to Mars, without humans on board. This **probe**, called Mars Express will **orbit** above the surface of Mars to find out lots of information without risking any human life. Mars Express is designed to be low cost, quick and efficient. Its tasks are to look for water below the Martian surface, to analyse the **atmosphere** and to look at the **geology** of Mars. All these things are important if we are to send people to live on Mars.

MISSION TASK

When choosing when to launch a mission to Mars, you must find out when Mars and Earth are close together, so your probe travels the least amount of distance.

1) You decide to launch the probe exactly 100 days before the date when Mars and Earth are at their closest. Use the dates in the DATA BOX on page 9. You may also want to look at the calendar on page 28. Give the date of launch you would choose if you were intending to land a probe on Mars in:
   a) 2010
   b) 2012

2) Look at your answers from Question 1. If the journey took exactly 6 calendar months, what date would the probe arrive at Mars?

(You will find a TIP to help you with these questions on page 28)

The Mars Express probe orbits above the planet, collecting data.

MARS EXPRESS FACTS

The Mars Express has **solar panels** to provide it with the energy it needs. The panels charge batteries, which keep the probe working even when it goes into darkness as it travels around Mars on the opposite side to the Sun.
The solar panels are folded up when the rocket is launched. After the probe has separated from the rocket they are opened and turned to face the Sun one at a time. The area of the solar panels is 11.42 m^2 and they can generate 650 watts of electricity.

DATA BOX # THE ORBITS OF MARS AND EARTH

All planets revolve around the Sun. We say that the planets orbit the Sun. An orbit is the path something takes as it moves around another object.

The Earth takes about 365 days to orbit the sun. Mars takes 687 days. Because the Earth and Mars take a different length of time to orbit the Sun the two planets are sometimes close to each other and sometimes far apart as these diagrams show.

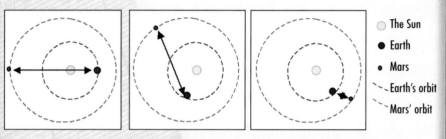

○ The Sun
● Earth
• Mars
~ Earth's orbit
~ Mars' orbit

The Mars Express mission must be timed to coincide with the time when Mars is at its closest point to Earth. In 2003, when Mars was very close to the Earth it was about 55 million kilometres away. Sometimes Mars can be as much as 400 million kilometres away! It takes the Earth and Mars just over 2 years and 1 month (about 765 days) to get close to each other again.

These are some of the dates when Mars is closest to the Earth:

December	January	March	April
23	**27**	**4**	**10**
2007	2010	2012	2014

CHALLENGE QUESTION
In the DATA BOX above you will see the number of days it takes Mars and the Earth to orbit the Sun once.

How many days does it take for:
a) Earth to orbit the Sun twice?
b) Mars to orbit the Sun twice?
c) Earth to orbit the Sun three times?
d) Mars to orbit the Sun three times?

TAKE OFF!

The day has arrived – Mars Express is due to be launched. The countdown begins 12 hours before the launch and there are many things to be tested and monitored before lift-off. A launch countdown is planned carefully so that there is time to check everything, and everyone is clear about the things that should happen. The countdown ensures the tests are carried out in the right order. You are asked to help with the final countdown by making sure that each thing happens on time. As the countdown reaches its end, everyone waits nervously to see if the rocket will take off successfully.

MISSION TASK

In the DATA BOX on page 11 you will see the launch countdown, beginning 12 hours before the launch. Make sure you know what times each of the stages should take place.

1) If the launch time was to be exactly 17:25 what time would each of these stages take place?
   a) Stage 1   f) Stage 6
   b) Stage 2   g) Stage 7
   c) Stage 3   h) Stage 8
   d) Stage 4   i) Stage 9
   e) Stage 5

2) You have been given the job of counting down progress on several tasks. You will need to count backwards in different sized steps. Can you say what the next three numbers in each of these sequences would be?
   a) 18, 16, 14, 12, 10
   b) 42, 37, 32, 27, 22, 17
   c) 24, 21, 18, 15, 12
   d) 29.5, 25.5, 21.5, 17.5, 13.5
   e) 9.8, 8.7, 7.6, 6.5, 5.4, 4.3

(You will find TIPS to help you with these questions on page 28)

DATA BOX

LAUNCH COUNTDOWN

Stage	Time	Event
1	-12h 00m 00s	Start of final countdown
2	- 7h 30m 00s	Check of electrical systems
3	- 3h 20m 00s	Chilldown of main engine
4	- 1h 10m 00s	Check of connections between launcher and command systems
5	-7m 00s	All systems go report, allowing start of sequence
6	-4m 00s	Tanks pressurized for flight
7	-1m 00s	Switch to onboard power mode
8	-04s	Onboard systems take over
9	-03s	Unlocking of guidance systems to flight mode
LAUNCH!	00s	Ignition of the main engine

Mars Express was launched with the Soyuz rocket.

CHALLENGE QUESTION

In the Rocket Facts box you will see that a rocket has to travel at 8 km a second to go into **orbit**.

If the rocket continued to travel at this speed, how far would it travel in:

a) 2 seconds?
b) 10 seconds?
c) 30 seconds?
d) 1 minute?
e) 5 minutes?
f) 10 minutes?
g) 30 minutes?
h) 1 hour?
i) 1 day?

(You will find a TIP to help you with this question on page 28)

ROCKET FACTS

The rocket must use enormous power to achieve what is known as '**escape velocity**'. This is the **speed** at which the rocket must be travelling to get away from the Earth's pull of **gravity**. Gravity is the force that tends to pull things toward the centre of a planet. To go into orbit the rocket has to travel at a speed of 8 kilometres per second. This means that the rocket travels 8 kilometres (8000 metres) in one second. This is 100 times faster than a racing car can travel.

MISSION CONTROL

Back on Earth you are standing at the Mission Control for Mars Express. This is the centre where every part of the **probe's** journey to Mars is monitored and altered, if necessary. The Mission Control room is full of screens showing different pieces of information about the probe. Mars Express continuously sends millions of bits of data back to the ground station. They show the planet in unique detail. From the raw data countless evaluations are made. This will help scientists unveil the secrets of the planet and its **atmosphere.** You need to be sure that you can read all the data shown and interpret what it means.

MISSION TASK

Look at these dials and scales shown on the screens at **ground control.**

Can you work out the number each red arrow is pointing to?

Speedometer (km/h)   **Mass**   **Angular momentum**

29000

a →

c

0.4

0.2   0.6

g

0   0.8

b →

28000

12

6

0   ← d

-6

-12   ← e

Spacecraft acceleration (km/m²)

-50   -25   0   25   50

f

g

(You will find a TIP to help you with this question on page 28)

Scientists at the Mission Control Centre monitor the probe on Mars 24 hours a day.

Mars Express has sent back this photo of part of surface of Mars. Each square is about 15 km across.

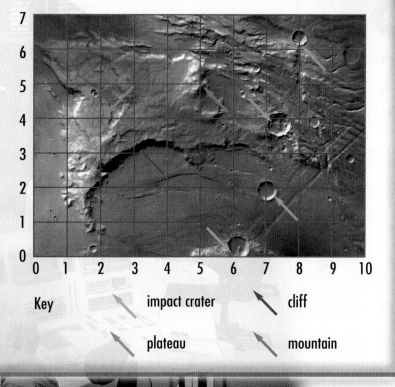

Key — impact crater — cliff

plateau — mountain

CHALLENGE QUESTIONS

It is very important that everyone at ground control analyses and records all the information carefully and correctly. Look at the DATA BOX above. The graph shows a photo of part of the surface of Mars.

1) Can you identify the missing **coordinates** to match each of these features on the photograph?

   a) There are large impact craters at (6,0) (7, ...) and near (7, ...) and (8, ...)

   b) There is a large circular plateau that can be found near (2, ...)

   c) The tallest cliff in this photo is found near (3, ...)

   d) The highest mountain peak in this photo is found near (....., 5)

2) What is the distance in kilometres between:

   a) (4, 1) and (4, 6)?

   b) (1, 1) and (9, 1)?

   c) (3, 5) and (9, 5)?

(You will find a TIP to help you with these questions on page 28)

THE PROBE ON MARS

Six months after its launch, the Mars Express has safely reached Mars. It remains in **orbit** above the planet while a **probe** is sent down to the surface. Now it is time for you to use the scientific instruments to direct the probe to collect information about the surface of Mars. You must try to find out about the **temperature** of Mars at different parts of its surface. You need to find out about the **atmosphere** – is there oxygen that humans could breathe? What is the **geology** like? How much **gravity** is there? You also need the probe to take photos and plot maps of the planet's surface. There is a lot to do!

MISSION TASK

You will need to understand the rise and fall in temperatures on the surface of Mars.

Answer these questions:

1) At the south pole of Mars, the temperature was -80°C and it rose by 65°C. What is the new temperature?

2) In the summer the daytime temperature was 8°C and it fell by 50°C. What is the new temperature?

3) Find the new temperatures for each of these situations:

a) The temperature was -2°C and fell by 28°C.

b) The temperature was -3°C, rose by 7°C and then rose again by 6°C.

c) The temperature was -15°C, fell by 28°C and then rose by 13°C.

d) The temperature was -75°C, rose by 22°C, rose by 26°C and then fell by 14°C.

(You will find a TIP to help you with these questions on page 29)

An artist's impression of a probe as it begins its exploration of Mars.

The probe has collected lots of data about the temperature of Mars. From these measurements you can find out the highest and lowest temperatures of different places on the surface:

Maximum temperature: 27°C (daytime at the equator in summer)
Minimum temperature: -133°C (night-time at the north pole in winter)

You discover there is a difference between the temperature on the ground and the temperature 1 metre above the ground. Sometimes this difference can be as much as 15°C.

The graph below shows two sets of temperatures on Mars, one taken 1 metre above the ground (the pink line) and one taken 25 cm above the ground (the blue line).

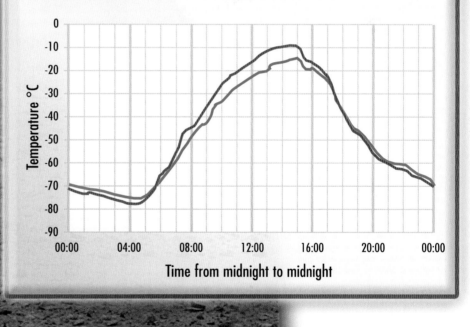

CHALLENGE QUESTIONS

Look carefully at the line graph in the DATA BOX above.
Which of these statements are true and which are false?

1) The temperature at 12:00 midday is warmer at 1 metre above the ground than at 25 cm above the ground.
2) The temperature at 18:00 is the same at 1 metre above the ground as it is at 25 cm above the ground.
3) The temperature at 4 a.m. is colder at 1 metre above the ground than at 25 cm above the ground.
4) The highest recorded temperature is about -12°C.
5) The lowest recorded temperature is about -77°C.
6) The lowest temperature was recorded at about 2 a.m.

CONCORDIA

Now that you are receiving information about how cold it is on Mars you decide that some more research is necessary. To see how humans cope with being in conditions that are very cold and dark for long periods, you decide to send a team of people to the space research centre in the Antarctic, called Concordia. In Concordia in the winter there is less than one hour of sunlight each day for several months and the **temperatures** plummet to as low as -85°C. Here you can monitor how people will survive in such conditions. How will they keep fit? What can we learn about how people might survive on Mars?

Concordia is a permanent research station in Antarctica.

MISSION TASK

In the DATA BOX on page 17 you will see a table showing the temperatures and wind **speeds** at the Concordia station. Use the table to help you answer these questions:

1) In which month or months is the:
   a) coldest average air temperature?
   b) warmest average air temperature?
   c) highest maximum air temperature?
   d) lowest minimum air temperature?
   e) fastest average wind speed?
   f) slowest average wind speed?
   g) fastest maximum wind speed?

2) What is the **difference** between the maximum and minimum air temperatures in:
   a) April?
   b) August?
   c) June?

3) How many more metres per second (m/s) faster is the average wind speed in:
   a) April than in August?
   b) June than in March?
   c) October than in February?

RESEARCH FACTS

Concordia is very remote and isolated. This isolation makes it ideal for testing equipment and procedures for future work on planets and the moon.

It is also excellent for understanding behaviour of small groups of people in small confined spaces for long periods of time, like a spacecraft, a space station or a planet/moon base.

There are about 16 people who work at the station in the winter and about 32 in the summer months. These include 9 scientists, 4 technicians, a chief chef, an assistant cook and a doctor.

CONCORDIA FACTS

In winter, the station at Concordia is composed of 3 buildings linked by walk ways. The quiet building contains sleeping quarters, laboratories and a hospital. A 'noisier' building has a workshop, waste water recycling plant, communications room, kitchen and restaurant. The third building has a boiler room, generator and another workshop.

DATA BOX   CONCORDIA STATISTICS

The table below shows the temperatures and wind **speed** in the Antarctic, at the Concordia station during one year. The orange rows in the table are the summer months and the blue rows are the winter months, when there is less than one hour's sunlight.

Month	Average air temp (°C)	Maximum air temp (°C)	Minimum air temp (°C)	Average wind speed (m/s)	Maximum wind speed (m/s)
Jan	-28.6	-16	-45	3	8
Feb	-41.8	-17	-57.9	1.8	6
Mar	-55.7	-29.6	-69	2.4	9
Apr	-60.7	-44	-71	2.4	9
May	-65.2	-31.2	-80	2.9	12
Jun	-61	-41.9	-77.9	3.1	11
Jul	-60.7	-37.8	-73.2	2.6	10
Aug	-67.8	-46	-80	1.9	7
Sep	-56.5	-29.6	-75.6	2.5	10
Oct	-50.6	-31.4	-67.1	2.8	12
Nov	-38.2	-13.4	-62	2.3	10
Dec	-31.3	-17	-44.5	2.2	8

CHALLENGE QUESTIONS

The mean of the average air temperatures for the whole year can be found by adding all the average air temperatures for each month and then dividing by 12 (the number of months).

1) Find the mean average air temperature for the year. Round your answer to the nearest tenth (to one decimal place). Use a calculator to help you work out the answer.

2) Now find the mean average wind speed for the year.

(You will find a TIP to help you with these questions on page 29)

THE INTERNATIONAL SPACE STATION

The information from Concordia can help you to monitor how humans might cope in cold, dark conditions for long periods of time. But it cannot help you to find out about how humans would cope with being in space. You will need to find out whether people find it stressful to live in weightless conditions, and how to prevent the **deterioration** of bones and muscles. The **International Space Station** (ISS) was set up to collect information for long missions in space. It is a place outside the Earth's **atmosphere** where teams of researchers can live for months at a time. You decide to go there to find out about what life is like in space.

MISSION TASK

In the DATA BOX on page 19 you will see information about the weight of a person on different planets and on the Sun and the Moon.

On Earth, a person weighs 50kg. How much would that person weigh on:

a) Jupiter   f) Mars
b) Neptune   g) Mercury
c) Saturn   h) Pluto
d) Uranus   i) the Sun
e) Venus   j) the Moon

(You will find a TIP to help you with this question on page 29)

SPACE TOILET FACTS

Space toilets do not use water. Instead, **astronauts** must first fasten themselves to the toilet seat. A lever operates a powerful fan and a suction hole slides open: the air stream carries the waste neatly away. Some crew members find the toilet difficult to get used to. As well as the device itself, they have to get used to the strange fact that their bowels actually float inside their bodies - like the rest of their internal organs and of course everything else on board.

ISS FACTS

- The ISS travels around the Earth about 400 km above our heads.
- It orbits the Earth at 28 000 km per hour, which is about 7.8 km every second.
- The ISS takes only 1.5 hours to orbit the Earth.

DATA BOX GRAVITY

A person's weight changes as they go to different planets, as **gravity** is different on each planet.

On Jupiter a person's weight is about 2.63 times their weight on Earth.
On Mars a person's weight is about 0.38 times their weight on Earth.
On Mercury a person's weight is about 0.34 times their weight on Earth.
On Neptune a person's weight is about 1.4 times their weight on Earth.
On Pluto a person's weight is about 0.13 times their weight on Earth.
On Saturn a person's weight is about 1.13 times their weight on Earth.
On Uranus a person's weight is about 1.06 times their weight on Earth.
On Venus a person's weight is about 0.87 times their weight on Earth.

On the Sun a person's weight would be about 279 times their weight on Earth.
On the Moon a person's weight is about 0.17 times their weight on Earth.

An artist's impression of how the International Space Station looks from space.

CHALLENGE QUESTIONS

The ISS **orbits** the Earth at 28 000 km per hour. To help you understand how fast this is, you can compare it with other moving objects. You will need a calculator to answer these questions. Round your answers to the nearest whole number.

A person walks at 8 km per hour. This is 8000 metres per hour, 133 metres per minute and 2 metres per second. Now try these questions:

1) A person runs at 12 km per hour. What is this in
   a) metres per hour?   b) metres per minute?   c) metres per second?
2) A car on a motorway travels at 108 km per hour. What is this in
   a) metres per hour?   b) metres per minute?   c) metres per second?
3) An express train travels at 240 km per hour. What is this in
   a) metres per hour?   b) metres per minute?   c) metres per second?
4) An aeroplane travels at 960 km per hour. What is this in
   a) metres per hour?   b) metres per minute?   c) metres per second?
5) The ISS travels at 28000 km per hour. What is this in
   a) metres per hour?   b) metres per minute?   c) metres per second?

(You will find a TIP to help you with these questions on page 29)

THE DAILY ROUTINE

You are settling in to life aboard the **International Space Station**. Your first duty is maintenance to the station. This includes cleaning, vacuuming to clean dust from air and surfaces, cleaning filters and installing and upgrading software. You spend a lot of time exercising. Muscles **deteriorate** when there is no or little **gravity**, so forcing your muscles to work prevents weakness. Finally, you must monitor and check the scientific experiments. Some experiments require **astronauts** to work with chemicals or conduct delicate crystal growing experiments. There's plenty to keep you busy during the six months you will be on the ISS.

MISSION TASK

The DATA BOX on page 21 shows how astronauts spend their time.

1) How many hours a week does an astronaut usually work?
2) How many minutes is this?
2) What percentage of time on shift is not spent on maintenance, exercise or research?
3) Write each of these percentages as a fraction in its simplest form.
   a) 20%   b) 30%   c) 25%

(You will find TIPS to help you with these questions on page 29)

The astronaut Sergei Krikalev exercises on the Treadmill Vibration Isolation System (TVIS).

DON'T LEAVE!

What would happen if you stepped outside the ISS without a space suit?

- You would lose consciousness because there is no oxygen. This could occur in as little as 15 seconds. Death would follow quickly.
- Because there is no air pressure to keep your blood and body fluids in a liquid state, the fluids would "boil." Then the fluids would freeze before they were evaporated totally. This all could take from 30 seconds to 1 minute.
- Your skin, heart, other internal organs would expand because of the boiling fluids.
- You would face extreme changes in temperature from 120°C in sunlight to -100°C in the shade.
- You would be exposed to various types of radiation (**cosmic rays**) or charged particles emitted from the Sun (solar wind).
- You could be hit by particles of dust or rock that move at high speeds or orbiting debris from **satellites** or spacecraft.

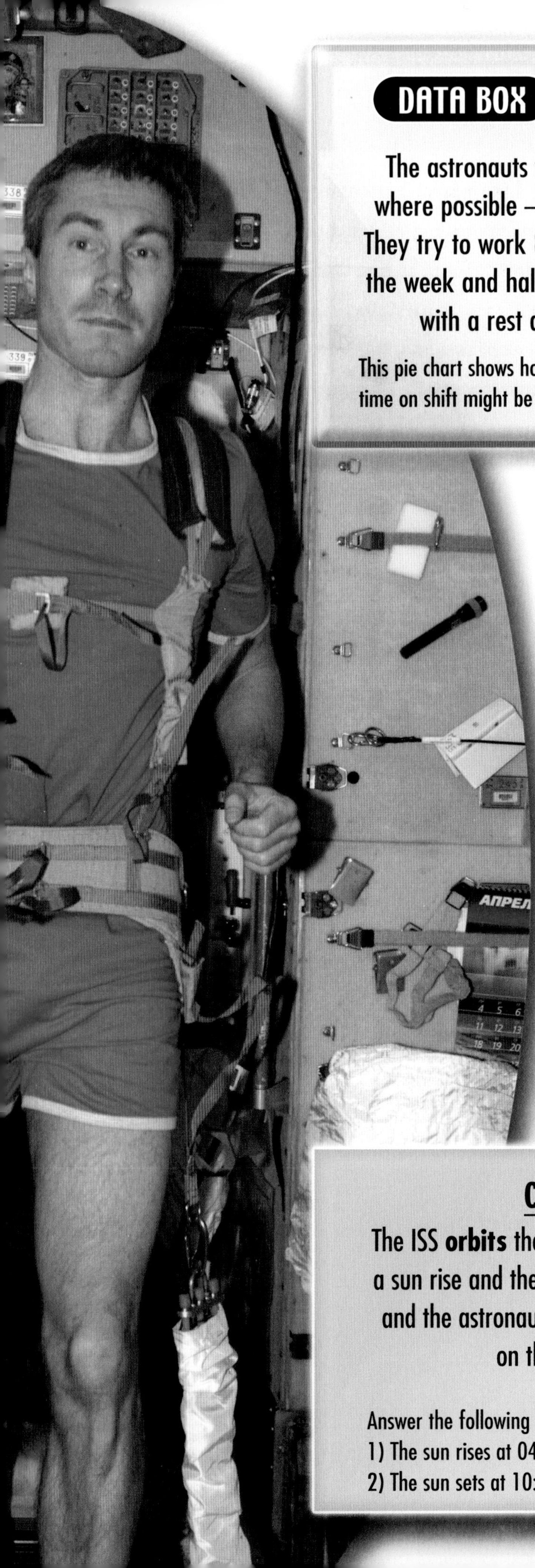

DATA BOX THE ISS DAY

The astronauts work regular hours where possible – just like on Earth. They try to work 8 hour shifts during the week and half days on Saturday, with a rest day on Sunday.

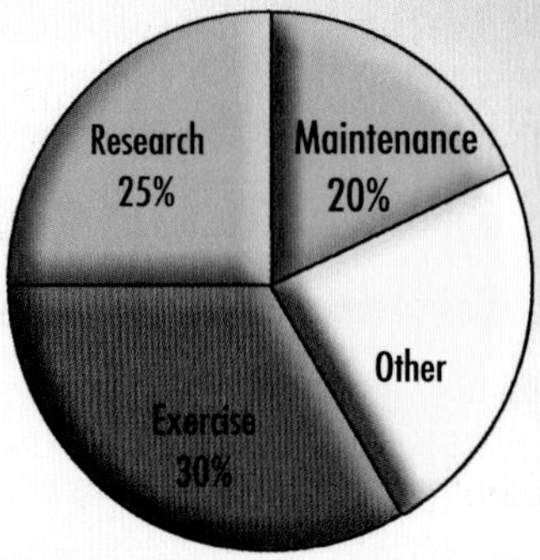

This pie chart shows how an astronaut's time on shift might be spent.

Pie chart labels:
Research 25%
Maintenance 20%
Other
Exercise 30%

The astronaut Claudie Haigneré spent a week on the International Space Station.

CHALLENGE QUESTIONS

The ISS **orbits** the Earth every hour and a half. The astronauts see a sun rise and then have 45 minutes of daylight. Then the sun sets and the astronauts have 45 minutes of darkness, when the ISS is on the other side of Earth from the Sun.

Answer the following questions using the 24 hour clock.
1) The sun rises at 04.47. List the times of the next three sun rises you will see.
2) The sun sets at 10:02. List the times of the next three sunsets you will see.

FOOD AND WATER ON THE ISS

Have you ever thought about what you might eat and drink in space? You are staying at the **ISS** for up to 6 months. Where will the food come from? There is no refrigerator on board so all foods are canned, **dehydrated,** or otherwise packaged so that they don't need to be kept cold. The food comes in containers that can be thrown away, so no washing up is necessary. Space station crew members have three meals a day. Drinks on the ISS are in powdered form and crew members have only lukewarm, warm and hot water to make the drinks with. No cold water is available. The **astronauts** usually eat breakfast and dinner together.

MISSION TASK

In the DATA BOX on page 23 you will see a list of one day's food. This is Menu 1.

The menu is repeated every 8 days for the length of the mission, which is 60 days. Continue the next numbers in each sequence to show which days the astronaut will eat the same foods.

1) a) Menu 1 served on days 1, 9, 17, 25 ......
   b) Menu 3 served on days 3, 11, 19, 27 ......
   c) Menu 6 served on days 6, 14, 22, 30 ......
   d) Menu 8 served on days 8, 16, 24, 32......

2) Menu 1 was eaten by an astronaut on the 19th October. Give the next 6 dates when the astronaut would eat the same food.

(If you need help with Question 2, look at the calendar on page 28)

Food floating on board the ISS

WATER FACTS

Besides air, water is the most important element aboard the ISS. Initially, water was brought from Earth, but it has to be carefully conserved. There are no long, luxurious showers on board. In fact, most astronauts get by with sponge baths. The water recovery system will collect, recycle and distribute water from:
- the sink and shower
- waste produced by the astronauts and laboratory animals (from urine and moisture breathed out)
- heating and cooling systems, including the water in **spacesuits**
- the space shuttle's fuel cells

WHICH MENU?

A menu is repeated every 8 days. To find out which menu will be served on a certain day, divide the number of days by 8 and find the remainder. Use this key:

Remainder 0: Menu 8
Remainder 1: Menu 1
Remainder 2: Menu 2
Remainder 3: Menu 3
Remainder 4: Menu 4
Remainder 5: Menu 5
Remainder 6: Menu 6
Remainder 7: Menu 7

THE MENU

Below is an example of one astronaut's daily menu.

You will need to understand these words:

Rehydratable foods require water to be added to them before eating.

Thermostabilization is when food is preserved by heat, which destroys all micro-organisms.

Intermediate Moisture is when foods are packaged with some, but not all, moisture removed.

MENU FOR DAY 1

Breakfast
Cottage cheese with nuts (rehydratable)
Oatmeal with peaches (rehydratable)
Plum-cherry dessert (intermediate moisture)
Coffee with sugar

Midday Meal
Grilled chicken (thermostabilized)
Rice with butter (thermostabilized)
Creamed spinach (rehydratable)
Pineapple (thermostabilized)
Grapefruit drink

Evening Meal
Chicken fajitas (thermostabilized)
Tortillas
Sweetcorn (thermostabilized)
Apples with spice (thermostabilized)
Brownie
Peach-apricot drink

Supper
Dried pears (intermediate moisture)
Nuts
Orange-pineapple drink

CHALLENGE QUESTION

Look at DATA BOX 2 on page 23.

Which menu will be served on day:
a) 50?
b) 36?
c) 23?
d) 53?
e) 59?

MISSION TO MARS

Now that you have gathered data from the Mars Express, from Concordia and from the **ISS**, you can start thinking about a manned mission to Mars. The trip is likely to take at least two years, so you will need to plan the mission carefully. The spacecraft cannot carry enough food, water and air for each person for two years, so you will need to find ways to recycle air and water, and grow food. The **astronauts** on the mission will be the first people to ever step on to a new planet. To send them 60 million km into space – and bring them back safely – will be one of the most impressive achievements in human history.

MISSION TASK

It's the year 2030 and astronauts are just about to land on Mars. The newspapers are full of stories about what might happen. You rate each story by how likely it is to happen.

a) Find Mars is made of red cheese   impossible
b) Land in correct area   likely
c) Discover Mars once had water   even chance
d) Landing damages spacecraft   unlikely
e) Astronauts sulk and refuse to go out   very unlikely
f) Astronauts are first people on Mars   certain
g) Discover Mars once had life   unlikely
h) Bring back rocks never seen on Earth   very likely

Probabilities can be shown on a probability scale from impossible to certain. Decide where each story should go on this scale.

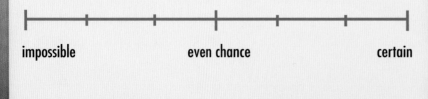

impossible   even chance   certain

(You will find a TIP to help you with this question on page 29)

(You will find a TIP to help you with this question on page 29)

An artist's impression of how a base on Mars might look.

MARS SAMPLE RETURN

NASA is planning several missions to Mars. One of the most exciting is The Mars Sample Return project, due to be launched in the next 10–15 years. It will bring back rocks from Mars to Earth so scientists can study them in detail.

Your Mars **probe** collected rocks from four different sites. Once back on Earth, these rocks were distributed to space agencies around the world for further study.
The table shows how many rocks were collected from each site, and where they went.

	Site 1	Site 2	Site 3	Site 4
NASA	3	5	7	2
European Space Agency	0	2	3	1
Japan Aerospace Exploration Agency	4	1	3	2
Russian Aviation and Space Agency	3	4	4	1
Indian Space Research Organisation	1	1	1	0

CHALLENGE QUESTIONS

Look at the table in the DATA BOX on page 25 and answer these questions.

1) How many rocks is NASA studying?
2) How many rocks were collected from Site 2?
3) Which site were most rocks collected from?
4) How many more rocks is Russia studying than India?
5) How many rocks were collected in total?

BECOMING AN ASTRONAUT

I t still might be years before scientists can send people to Mars, but it will happen one day. Will you be the first astronaut to visit another planet? If you want to take part in a mission to Mars, the first step is to gain experience as an **astronaut**. It won't be easy! There are very few places and lots of competition. If you're one of the lucky ones, you will be given a unique opportunity to see our planet from space, and to experience the fun of freefall. Once you get back you will recover quickly from the effects of weightlessness – although some astronauts get so used to freefall that they simply let go of objects back on Earth and are surprised at the crash!

MISSION TASK

People have predicted that humans will walk on Mars by 2030. Most astronauts are aged between 28 and 40 years old.

Work out how old each of these people will be in the year 2030 and whether they would be the right age to be an astronaut in 2030.

I was born in 1999 — Amy

I was born in 2004 — Bethany

I was born in 2001 — Callum

I was born in 1992 — Daisy

I was born in 1989 — Emily

I was born in 1973 — Finlay

Are YOU the right age to be an astronaut in 2030?

SPACESUIT FACTS

To protect you from dangers, a **spacesuit** must:

- Have a pressurized **atmosphere**
- Give you oxygen and remove carbon dioxide
- Keep the temperature comfortable despite strenuous work and movement into and out of sunlit areas
- Protect you from micrometeoroids and from radiation
- Let you see clearly
- Allow you to move your body easily inside the spacesuit
- Let you talk with others (ground controllers, other astronauts)

Water is pumped around the space suit to keep the asronaut cool. The pump and water come from the pack on the back of the suit.

HOW TO BECOME AN ASTRONAUT

Well, it won't be easy. But if you wanted to do something easy, you wouldn't want to become an astronaut. So what do you need?

1) You must have the right background. Many astronauts began as pilots in military airforces. Others have scientific backgrounds in physics, engineering or medicine.

2) Being an astronaut is hard work, so you must be healthy and physcially fit.

3) You must speak English well. Astronauts come from all over the world, but as they all speak English, they can communicate with each other.

4) On a space station you will live and work in a small area, so it's important to get on well with other people.

5) You must be determined and motivated to become an astronaut. You will spend hundreds or even thousands of hours training.

CHALLENGE QUESTION

Yuri Gagarin was the first human in space in the year 1961. If the first human to land on Mars was to land there in the year 2030, how long would there be between these two events?

a) Give your answer in years.
b) How many months is this?
c) About how many weeks is this?
d) Approximately how many days is this?

(You will find a TIP to help you with this question on page 29)

TIPS FOR MATHS SUCCESS

PAGES 6–7

Subtracting large numbers

To find the difference between two numbers, subtract one from the other. When subtracting numbers with lots of digits, make sure that you line all the digits up so that the units line up with the units, tens with the tens, hundreds with the hundreds and so on.

```
  2870
-  228
  2642
```

PAGES 8–9

You might find these calendar pages useful for working out the answers.

It is also useful to know that 98 days is 14 weeks.

SEPTEMBER						
					1	2
3	4	5	6	7	8	9
10	11	12	13	14	15	16
17	18	19	20	21	22	23
24	25	26	27	28	29	30
31						

OCTOBER						
1	2	3	4	5	6	7
8	9	10	11	12	13	14
15	16	17	18	19	20	21
22	23	24	25	26	27	28
29	30	31				

NOVEMBER						
			1	2	3	4
5	6	7	8	9	10	11
12	13	14	15	16	17	18
19	20	21	22	23	24	25
26	27	28	29	30		

DECEMBER						
					1	2
3	4	5	6	7	8	9
10	11	12	13	14	15	16
17	18	19	20	21	22	23
24	25	26	27	28	29	30
31						

JANUARY						
1	2	3	4	5	6	7
8	9	10	11	12	13	14
15	16	17	18	19	20	21
22	23	24	25	26	27	28
29	30	31				

FEBRUARY						
		1	2	3	4	5
6	7	8	9	10	11	12
13	14	15	16	17	18	19
20	21	22	23	24	25	26
27	28	29				

MARCH						
			1	2	3	4
5	6	7	8	9	10	11
12	13	14	15	16	17	18
19	20	21	22	23	24	25
26	27	28	29	30	31	

This calendar shows a leap year such as 2012.

PAGES 10–11

Time: Remember that there are 60 seconds in a minute and 60 minutes in an hour.

When continuing sequences, find the difference between the numbers next to each other and look for patterns.

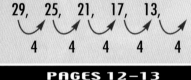

PAGES 12–13

Follow these steps when reading scales on measuring instruments:

Step 1: Choose two adjacent (next to each other) numbers and find the difference between them.

Step 2: Count how many small intervals (spaces) there are between these numbers.

Step 3: Work out, by dividing, how much each of these intervals is worth.

Each interval is worth 20, so the arrow is pointing to 440 (400 + 20 + 20).

CHALLENGE QUESTIONS

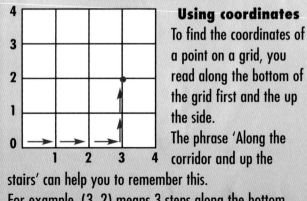

Using coordinates

To find the coordinates of a point on a grid, you read along the bottom of the grid first and the up the side.

The phrase 'Along the corridor and up the stairs' can help you to remember this.

For example, (3, 2) means 3 steps along the bottom and then 2 steps up.

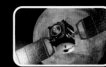

PAGES 14–15

Temperature

The temperature is how hot or cold something is. It is usually measured in degrees Celsius which are written using the symbols ˚C.

-70 -60 -50 -40 -30 -20 -10 0 10 20 30

When finding temperature rises, move to the right on the number line. If temperature falls, move to the left.

PAGES 16–17

CHALLENGE QUESTION

Rounding numbers up and down

Remember that the numbers 5, 6, 7, 8 or 9 round up and numbers ending in 1, 2, 3, 4 round down.

PAGES 18–19

When multiplying a number by 50 you can multiply it first by 100 and then halve the answer. To multiply a number by 100, move the digits two places to the left. We use zeros to fill any empty columns. For example, $0.8 \times 50 =$

$0.8 \times 100 = 80$

Tth	Th	H	T	U	.	t
				0	.	8
			8	0		

$80 \div 2 = 40$
so $0.8 \times 50 = 40$

CHALLENGE QUESTIONS

To change km per hour into metres per hour you will need to multiply by 1000.

To change metres per hour into metres per minute you will need to divide by 60.

To change metres per minute into metres per second you will need to divide by 60.

PAGES 20–21

Percentages

Percent (%) is a special form of a fraction and it means 'part of 100'. So 50% means $^{50}/_{100}$.

Fractions

A fraction in its simplest form cannot be made with smaller whole numbers on the top or bottom. So $^{50}/_{100}$ in it's simplest form is ½.

PAGES 24–25

Probability scale

To show a probability you can mark a cross on the line. The cross on this line shows a probability that is likely to happen.

very likely

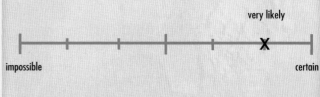

impossible   certain

PAGES 26–27

CHALLENGE QUESTION

To change a number of years into months, multiply the number of years by 12 as there are 12 months in each year.

To multiply by 12, first multiply the number by 10, then double the number and finally add your two answers together.

$47 \times 12 =$

$47 \times 10 = 470$
Double 47 $= 94$
$470 + 94 = 564$

So $47 \times 12 = 564$

ANSWERS ANSWERS ANSWERS

PAGES 6-7

MISSION TASK

1) a) 37
   b) 322

2) a) 2976
   b) 2981
   c) 1784

3) 3 times

CHALLENGE QUESTIONS

1) Mercury, Venus, Earth, Mars, Jupiter, Saturn, Uranus, Neptune, Pluto
2) Venus
3) a) 550 million km   b) 1199 million km
   c) 4269 million km
4) a) Jupiter   b) Mars   c) Pluto   d) Pluto

PAGES 8-9

MISSION TASK

1) a) 18th October 2009
   b) 23rd November 2011

2) a) 18th April 2010
   b) 23rd May 2012

CHALLENGE QUESTION

a) 730 days   c) 1095 days
b) 1374 days   d) 2061 days

PAGES 10-11

MISSION TASK

1) a) 05:25   f) 17:21
   b) 09:55   g) 17:24
   c) 14:05   h) 17:24 and 56 seconds
   d) 16:15   i) 17:24 and 57 seconds
   e) 17:18

2) a) 8, 6, 4   d) 9.5, 5.5, 1.5
   b) 12, 7, 2   e) 3.2, 2.1, 1
   c) 9, 6, 3

CHALLENGE QUESTION

a) 16 km   d) 480 km   g) 14 400 km
b) 80 km   e) 2400 km   h) 28 800 km
c) 240 km   f) 4800 km   i) 691 200 km

PAGES 12-13

MISSION TASK

a) 28 800   e) -9
b) 28 100   f) -10
c) 0.3   g) 40
d) 3

CHALLENGE QUESTIONS

1) a) (7, 2) (7, 4) (8, 6)   2) a) 75 km
   b) (2, 4)   b) 120 km
   c) (3, 3)   c) 90 km
   d) (5, 5)

PAGES 14-15

MISSION TASK

1) -15°C
2) -42°C
3) a) -30°C   c) -30°C
   b) 10°C   d) -41°C

CHALLENGE QUESTIONS

1) True   4) False – it's about -9°C
2) True   5) True
3) True   6) False – it's about 4 a.m.

PAGES 16-17

MISSION TASK

1) a) Aug   2) a) 27°C
   b) Jan   b) 34°C
   c) Nov   c) 36°C
   d) May and Aug
   e) Jun   3) a) 0.5
   f) Feb   b) 0.7
   g) May and Oct   c) 1

CHALLENGE QUESTIONS

1) -51.5°C
2) 2.5 m/s

ANSWERS ANSWERS ANSWERS

MISSION TASK

a) 131.5 kg	f) 19 kg
b) 70 kg	g) 17 kg
c) 56.5 kg	h) 6.5 kg
d) 53 kg	i) 13 950 kg
e) 43.5 kg	j) 8.5 kg

CHALLENGE QUESTIONS

1) a) 12 000 m
   b) 200 m
   c) 3 m
2) a) 108 000 m
   b) 1800 m
   c) 30 m
3) a) 240 000 m
   b) 4000 m
   c) 67 m
4) a) 960 000 m
   b) 16 000 m
   c) 267 m
5) a) 28 000 000 m
   b) 466 667 m
   c) 7778 m

MISSION TASK

1) 44 hours
2) 2640 minutes
3) 25%
4) a) $\frac{1}{5}$
   b) $\frac{3}{10}$
   c) $\frac{1}{4}$

CHALLENGE QUESTIONS

1) 06:17   07:47   09:17
2) 11:32   13:02   14:32

MISSION TASK

1) a) 33, 41, 49, 57
   b) 35, 43, 51, 59
   c) 38, 46, 54
   d) 40, 48, 56
2) 27th October, 4th November, 12th November, 20th November, 28th November and 6th December

CHALLENGE QUESTION

a) Menu 2	d) Menu 5
b) Menu 4	e) Menu 3
c) Menu 7	

MISSION TASK

CHALLENGE QUESTIONS

1) 17	4) 9
2) 13	5) 48
3) Site 3	

MISSION TASK

Amy	31	could be an astronaut
Bethany	26	too young to be an astronaut
Callum	29	could be an astronaut
Daisy	38	could be an astronaut
Emily	41	too old to be an astronaut
Finlay	57	too old to be an astronaut

CHALLENGE QUESTION

a) 69 years	c) about 3588 weeks
b) 828 months	d) about 25 000 days

31

GLOSSARY

ATMOSPHERE The air surrounding a planet.

ASTRONAUT A person who travels into space.

CORE The inner layer of a planet. Earth has a liquid core, while the core of Mars is thought to be solid.

CORE RADIUS The distance from the centre of a planet to the edge of its core.

COSMIC RAYS A form of radiation from atomic particles travelling almost at the speed of light.

DETERIORATE Get steadily worse.

EQUATORIAL RADIUS The distance from the centre of a planet's core to a point on its equator.

ESCAPE VELOCITY The minimum speed at which the rocket must be travelling to get away from the Earth's pull of gravity.

GEOLOGY The study of a planet's structure, such as rocks and minerals.

GRAVITY The force that attracts masses towards each other and which tends to draw things toward the centre of a planet.

GROUND CONTROL The team of people on Earth monitoring and programming the probe.

INTERNATIONAL SPACE STATION (ISS) The ISS orbits the Earth. It is run by space agencies from Europe, the USA, Canada, Japan and Russia.

ORBIT The path an object takes as it moves around another object.

MICROMETEOROID A tiny rock moving through space.

PROBE An unmanned spacecraft which collects information about objects in space and sends it back to scientists on Earth.

POLAR RADIUS The distance from the centre of a planet's core to the North or the South Pole.

SATELLITE An object that orbits a planet or a moon.

SOLAR PANELS Solar panels are used to convert energy from sunlight into electricity.

SOLAR SYSTEM The planets that revolve around our Sun.

SPACESUIT A suit to allow an astronaut to survive in space.

MATHS GLOSSARY

COORDINATES Two numbers in brackets used to show position on a grid, such as (3, 2) which means 3 steps to the right and 2 up starting from (0, 0).

DEGREES The units used for measuring angles ° or temperatures °C.

DIFFERENCE The difference between two numbers can be found by subtracting the smaller number from the larger number.

ESTIMATE To find a number or amount that is close to an exact number.

FRACTIONS These are made when shapes or numbers are split into equal parts. For example, if a shape is cut into 6 equals parts each part is one sixth or ⅙.

NEGATIVE NUMBERS Numbers on the other side of zero from positive numbers, such as -4, -2, -12 etc. Temperatures below 0°C are negative numbers and show freezing conditions.

RADIUS The distance from the centre of a circle to its circumference, or the distance from the centre of a sphere to its face.

TEMPERATURE How hot or cold something is. It is usually measured in degrees Celsius (°C).

SPEED A measure of how fast something is moving.

PICTURE CREDITS
Front cover: ESA

pp6-7 (Mars) NASA, J. Bell (Cornell U.) and M. Wolff (SSI), pp6-7 (Earth) NASA, p6 (cutaway Mars) NASA – Goddard Space Flight Center; pp8-9 ESA-D.Ducros; pp10-11 ESA/Starsem; pp12-13 ESA, p13 ESA/DLR/FU Berlin (G. Neukum); pp14-15 ESA - AOES Medialab; pp16-17 ESA; pp18-19 (main picture) ESA - D.Ducros, p18 (astronaut) ESA/CNES; pp20-21 NASA; pp22-23 NASA; pp24-25 Pat Rawlings, NASA; pp26-27 NASA

Every effort has been made to trace the copyright holders, and we apologize in advance for any unintentional omissions. We would be pleased to insert the appropriate acknowledgements in any subsequent edition of this publication.